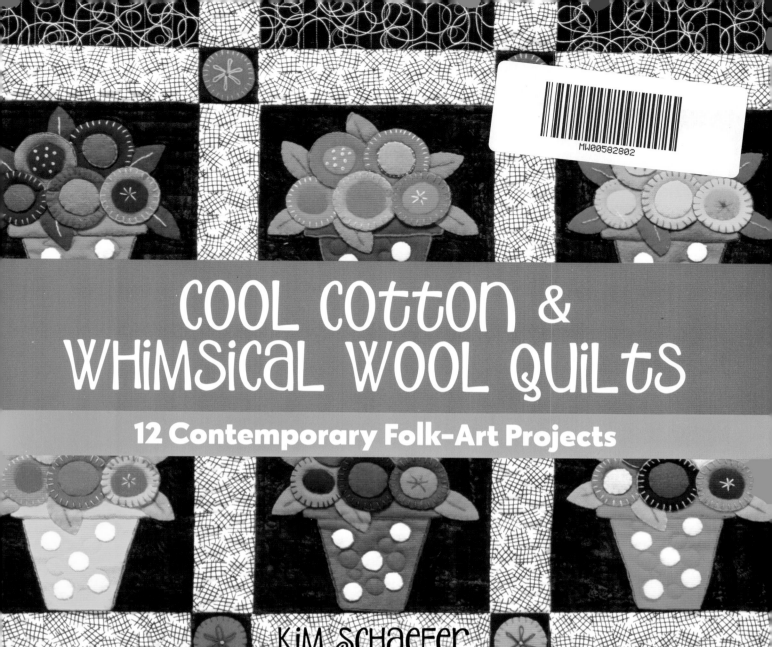

Cool Cotton & Whimsical Wool Quilts

12 Contemporary Folk-Art Projects

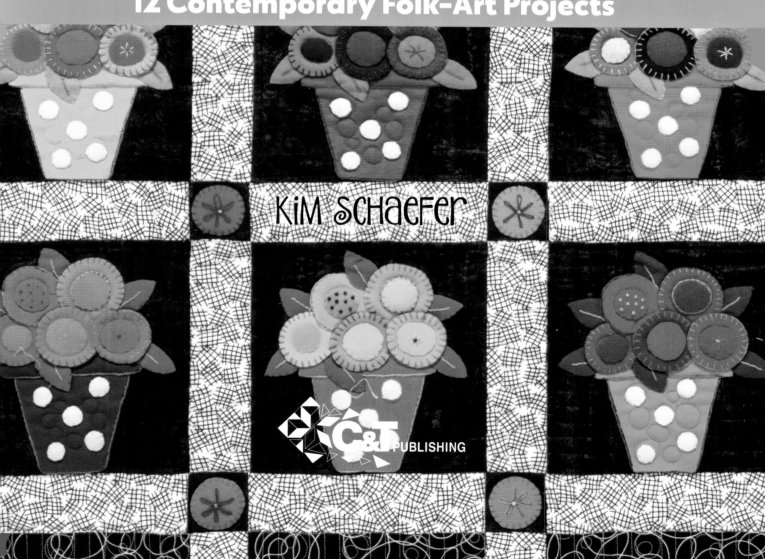

Kim Schaefer

C&T PUBLISHING

Publisher: Amy Barrett-Daffin

Creative Director: Gailen Runge

Acquisitions Editor: Roxane Cerda

Managing/Developmental Editor: Liz Aneloski

Technical Editor: Julie Waldman

Cover/Book Designer: April Mostek

Production Coordinator: Tim Manibusan

Production Editor: Alice Mace Nakanishi

Illustrator: Aliza Shalit

Photo Assistant: Gabriel Martinez

Photography by Estefany Gonzalez of C&T Publishing, Inc.,
unless otherwise noted

Published by C&T Publishing, Inc., P.O. Box 1456,
Lafayette, CA 94549

Library of Congress Cataloging-in-Publication Data

Names: Schaefer, Kim, 1960- author.

Title: Cool cotton & whimsical wool quilts : 12 contemporary
folk-art projects / Kim Schaefer.

Other titles: Cool cotton and whimsical wool quilts

Description: Lafayette, CA : C&T Publishing, [2021]

Identifiers: LCCN 2020055565 | ISBN 9781644030783
(trade paperback) | ISBN 9781644030790 (ebook)

Subjects: LCSH: Quilting--Patterns. | Appliqué--Patterns.

Classification: LCC TT835 .S28275 2021 | DDC 746.46/041--dc23

LC record available at https://lccn.loc.gov/2020055565

Printed in China

10 9 8 7 6 5 4 3 2 1

Acknowledgments

Special thanks to the following people:

Julie Waldman, my technical editor at C&T Publishing, for checking and rechecking the accuracy of my work.

Susan Lawson of Seamingly Slawson Quilts, for her incredible long arm quilting. I am so happy to have found you; your quilting is amazing.

Everyone at C&T Publishing for their continued support and encouragement.

My husband, Gary, for everything you do for me.

contents

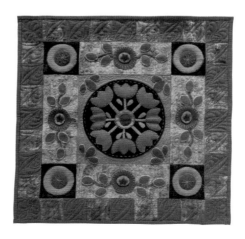

This book contains 12 projects all in my whimsical, contemporary, folk-art style. I worked on this book in the midst of the 2020 Coronavirus pandemic. It made me happy to design and stitch these projects. Whether you are an experienced stitcher or a beginner, I hope that the projects will inspire you to create. As always, with my work, it is my hope that I can bring a smile to my fellow stitchers and quilters.

General instructions

YARDAGE AND FABRIC REQUIREMENTS

I have given yardage and fabric requirements for each project. All the backgrounds in the projects are constructed using cotton fabrics, and the appliqué pieces are cut from felted wool.

The cotton fabric amounts are based on a usable width of 42″. Fusible web amounts are based on a width of 17″. The amounts given for binding allow for 2″-wide strips cut on the straight grain. I usually use the same fabric for backing and binding. It is a good way to use leftover fabric. Cut the binding strips on either the crosswise or lengthwise grain of the leftover fabric, whichever will yield the longest strips.

ROTARY CUTTING

I recommend that you cut all the fabrics used in the blocks, borders, and bindings with a rotary cutter, an acrylic ruler, and a cutting mat. Trim the blocks and borders with these tools as well.

PIECING

All piecing measurements include ¼″ seam allowances. If you sew an accurate ¼″ seam, you will succeed! My biggest and best quiltmaking tip is to learn to sew an accurate ¼″ seam.

PRESSING

For cotton fabrics, press the seams to one side, preferably toward the darker fabric. Press flat and avoid sliding the iron over the pieces, which can distort and stretch them. When you join two seamed sections, press the seams in opposite directions so you can nest the seams and reduce bulk.

APPLIQUÉ

All appliqué instructions are for paper-backed fusible web with hand stitching. All the projects could be done with machine appliqué as well, if you prefer. A lightweight paper-backed fusible web works best. Choose your favorite fusible web and follow the manufacturer's instructions.

General Appliqué Instructions

NOTE *The appliqué patterns in the book and on the pullout pages are given reversed, so the design will match the project photo after you trace them onto fusible web, fuse them to the fabric, cut them out, and fuse them to the background.*

1. Trace all parts of the appliqué design on the paper side of the fusible web.

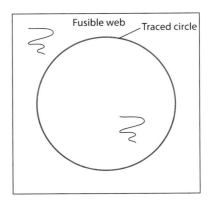

2. Trace each layer of the design separately. Whenever 2 shapes in the design butt together, overlap them by about ⅛″ to help prevent the potential of a gap between them. When tracing the shapes, extend the underlapped edge ⅛″ beyond the drawn edge in the pattern. Write the pattern letter or number on each traced shape.

3. Cut around the appliqué shapes, leaving a ¼˝ margin around each piece.

4. Iron each fusible web shape to the wrong side of the appropriate fabric, following the manufacturer's instructions for fusing. I don't worry about the grain-line when placing the pieces.

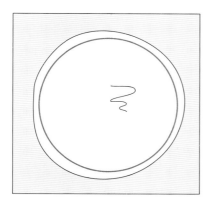

5. Cut on the traced lines and peel off the paper backing. A thin layer of fusible web will remain on the wrong side of the fabric. This layer will adhere the appliqué piece to the background.

6. Position the pieces on the backgrounds. Press to fuse them in place.

7. When hand stitching around the appliqué pieces, choose the stitch of your choice.

As a beginner to hand stitching, I chose the most basic of stitches (see The Stitches, page 8). If you are an experienced stitcher, I hope the blocks will inspire you to create some beautiful work. As always, the type of stitching you use and the thread colors you select are personal choices.

PUTTING IT ALL TOGETHER

When all the pieces are completed for a project, lay them out on the floor or, if you are lucky enough to have one, a design wall. Arrange and rearrange the pieces until you are happy with the overall look. Each project has specific instructions as well as diagrams and photos for assembly.

LAYERING THE QUILT

Cut the batting and backing pieces 4˝–5˝ larger than the quilt top. Place the pressed backing on the bottom, right side down. Place the batting over the backing and the quilt top on top, right side up. Make sure that all the layers are flat and smooth and that the quilt top is centered over the batting and backing. Pin or baste the quilt.

Note: If you are going to have your quilt quilted by a longarm quilter, contact them for specific batting and backing requirements, because they may differ from the instructions above.

QUILTING

Quilting is a personal choice; you may prefer hand or machine quilting. My favorite method is to send the quilt top to a longarm quilter. This method keeps my number of unfinished tops low and the number of finished quilts high.

THE STITCHES

As this book and collection of projects is for both beginners and experienced stitchers, I used the most basic of stitches.

Backstitch

Lazy Daisy

Blanket Stitch

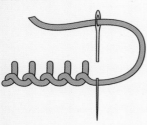

Running Stitch

Couching

Stem Stitch

Fly Stitch

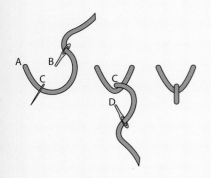

Whipstitch

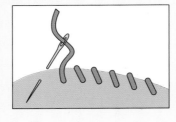

French Knot

Wrapped Backstitch

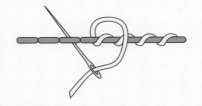

THE THREADS

There are a variety of beautiful threads available to hand stitchers. I kept to the basics.

- **60-weight 100% long staple Elfina Egyptian cotton** (by WonderFil Specialty Threads) for whipstitching the wool appliqué pieces to the background
- **Perle cotton #8** for blanket stitch, whipstitch, backstitch, wrapped backstitch, stem stitch, French knot, running stitch, and fly stitch
- **Perle cotton #3 and #5** for couching

THE NEEDLES

- **Milliners size 1** for French knots
- **Chenille size 24** for blanket stitch, whipstitch, backstitch, stem stitch, running stitch, and fly stitch
- **Chenille size 18** for wrapped backstitch
- **Appliqué size 10** for invisible whipstitch

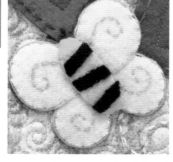

BUZZIN' AROUND

FINISHED WALL QUILT:
18½″ × 18½″

Made by Kim Schaefer,
quilted by Susan Lawson of
Seamingly Slawson Quilts

Two bees are buzzin' around
three modern flowers in
a rainbow of colors, all
surrounded by a black and
white border.

MATERIALS

Fabric

- 1 fat quarter of light blue cotton fabric for background
- ⅛ yard of white tone-on-tone cotton print for pieced border
- ⅛ yard of black tone-on-tone cotton print for pieced border

Felted wool

- 1 square 10″ × 10″ of black for flower centers and bee stripes
- Scraps in assorted teals, blues, purples, yellows, oranges, reds, pinks, and white for flower petals, bee, and bee wings

Other

- 22″ × 22″ of batting
- ¾ yard for backing and binding
- 1 yard of paper-backed fusible web
- Assorted threads for appliqué and embroidery

CUTTING

Blue fabric

• Cut 1 square 14½″ × 14½″.

White fabric

• Cut 16 squares 2½″ × 2½″.

Black fabric

• Cut 16 squares 2½″ × 2½″.

APPLIQUÉ

1. Refer to Appliqué (page 6) and the Buzzin' Around appliqué patterns (pages 11–14).

• Cut 1 each of pattern pieces 1–35.

• Cut 2 each of pattern pieces 36–40.

2. Appliqué the pieces onto the blue background.

BORDERS

1. Sew together 4 white squares and 3 black squares for each of the 2 side borders.

Piece 2 side borders.

2. Sew the 2 side borders to the quilt top. Press.

3. Sew together 5 black squares and 4 white squares for each of the top and bottom borders.

Piece top and bottom borders.

4. Sew the top and bottom borders to the quilt top. Press.

FINISHING

1. Layer the quilt top with batting and backing. Baste or pin.

2. Quilt as desired and bind.

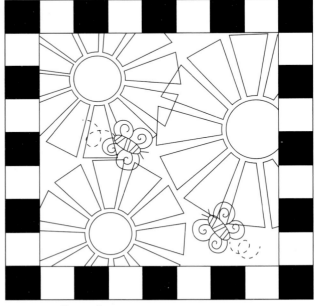

Putting it all together

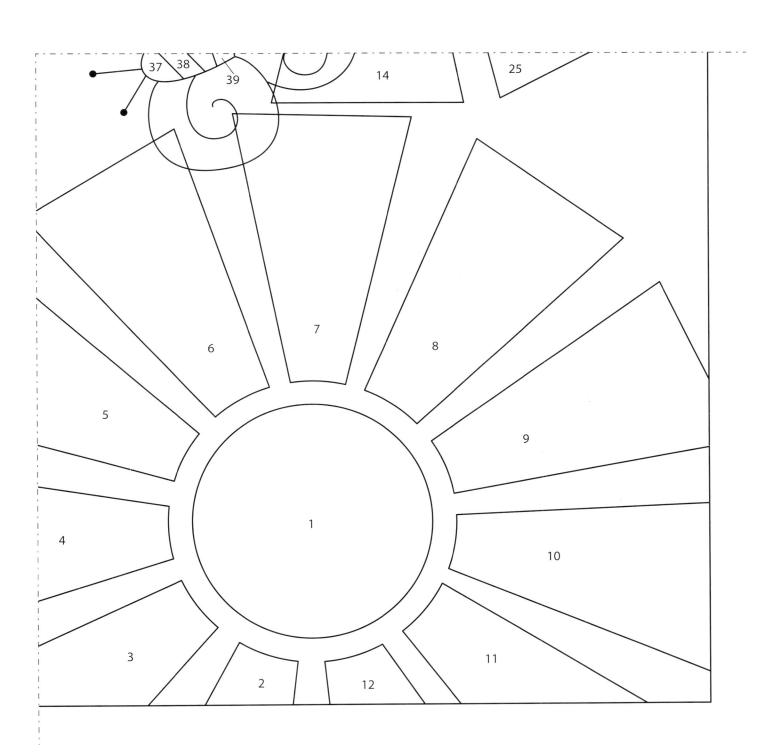

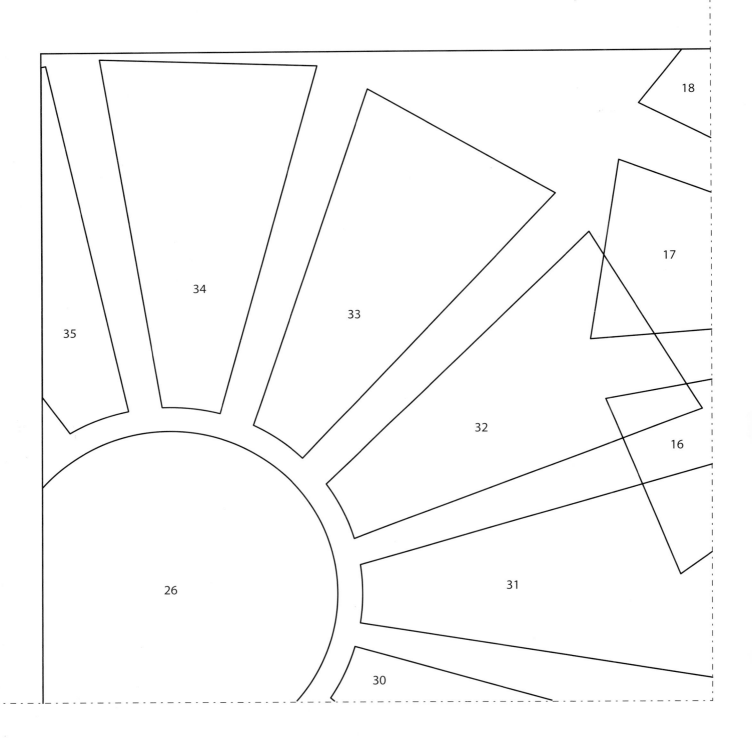

CHICKEN SCRATCH

FINISHED WALL QUILT:
16½″ × 16½″

Made by Kim Schaefer, quilted by Susan Lawson of Seamingly Slawson Quilts

This whimsical chicken is out enjoying the sun. The background and borders are made from Marcia Derse Fabrics.

MATERIALS

Fabric

- ½ yard of blue cotton fabric for background
- ¼ yard total of assorted bright cotton fabrics for pieced border

Felted wool

- 1 square 10″ × 10″ of black for chicken
- 1 square 5″ × 5″ of orange for chicken tail
- 1 square 5″ × 5″ of purple for chicken wing
- 1 square 5″ × 5″ of yellow for sun and sun rays
- 1 rectangle 4″ × 13″ of green for grass

Felted wool scraps

- Orange for beak and flowers
- Red for wattle and head feathers
- Green for stems, leaves, and dots on chicken wing
- 2 assorted pinks for flower
- Dark red for flower
- Peach for flower
- Blue for tail
- Dark purple for inside circles on chicken wing
- White for eye and chicken spots

Other

- 20″ × 20″ of batting
- ½ yard for backing and binding
- ½ yard of paper-backed fusible web
- Assorted threads for appliqué and embroidery

BORDERS

1. Sew together 6 assorted bright squares for each of the 2 side borders. Press.

Piece 2 side borders.

2. Sew the 2 side borders to the quilt top. Press.

3. Sew together 8 assorted bright squares for each of the top and bottom borders. Press.

Piece top and bottom borders.

4. Sew the top and bottom borders to the quilt top. Press.

FINISHING

1. Layer the quilt top with batting and backing. Baste or pin.

2. Quilt as desired and bind.

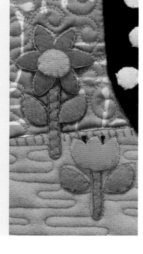

CUTTING

Blue fabric

• Cut 1 square 12½″ × 12½″.

Assorted brights

• Cut 28 squares 2½″ × 2½″.

APPLIQUÉ

1. Refer to Appliqué (page 6) and the Chicken Scratch appliqué patterns (pages 17–20).

• Cut 1 each of pattern pieces 1–50.

• Cut 17 of pattern piece 51.

2. Appliqué the pieces onto the blue background.

Putting it all together

1

4

2

3

5

51

20

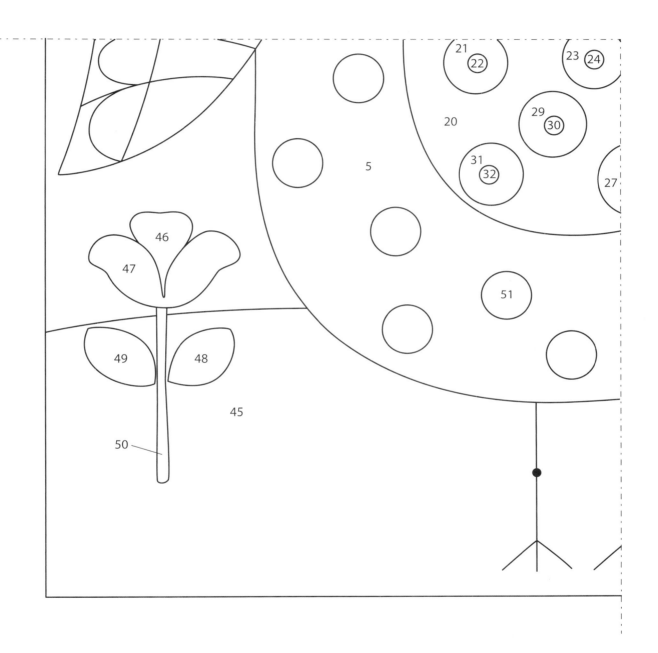

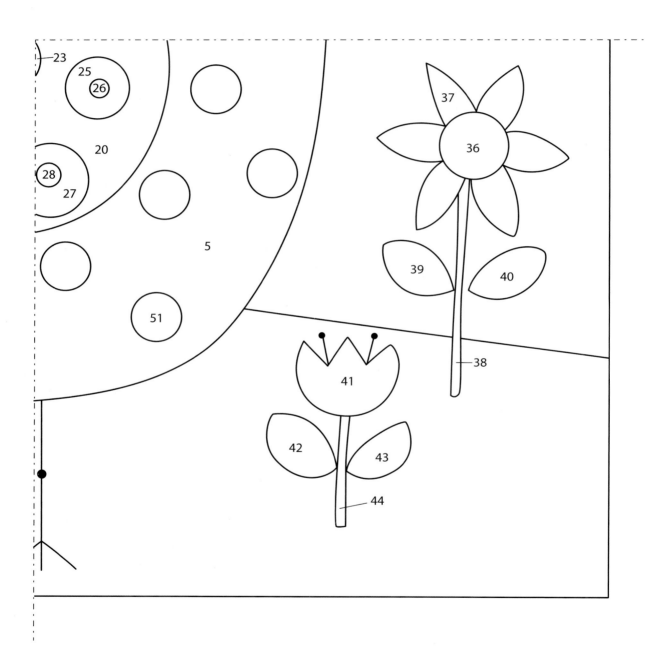

BiRDS OF A FeaTHeR

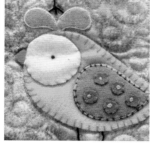

FINISHED WALL QUILT:
18½″ × 18½″

Made by Kim Schaefer,
quilted by Susan Lawson of
Seamingly Slawson Quilts

Stitch up a tower with
these whimsical birds and
butterflies.

MATERIALS

Fabric

• ⅝ yard of blue cotton fabric
for background

Felted wool

• 1 square 10″ × 10″ of green
for stems and leaves

• 1 square 5″ × 5″ of white
for bird eyes and bee wings

• 1 square 5″ × 5″ of red
for bird body

• 1 square 5″ × 5″ of yellow
for bird body and bee body

• 1 square 5″ × 5″ of dark purple
for bird body

Felted wool scraps

• 2 reds for bird wings and feathers

• 2 golds for bird wings and feathers

• Blue for dots

• 3 purples for bird wings and feathers

• 3 oranges for butterfly and beaks

• 3 pinks for butterfly

• 5 greens for leaves

• Black for butterfly bodies

Other

• 22″ × 22″ of batting

• ⅞ yard for backing and binding

• 1 yard of paper-backed fusible web

• Assorted threads for appliqué
and embroidery

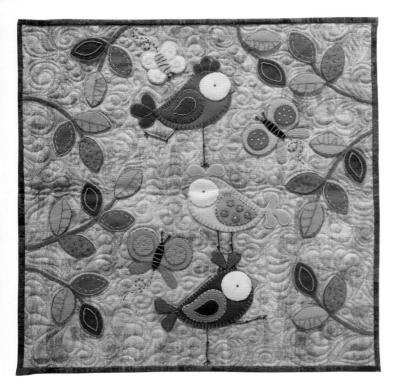

APPLIQUÉ

1. Refer to Appliqué (page 6) and the Birds of a Feather appliqué pattern (pullout page P1).

- Cut 1 each of pattern pieces 1–19.
- Cut 2 each of pattern pieces 20–26.
- Cut 3 of pattern piece 27.
- Cut 5 of pattern piece 28.
- Cut 27 of pattern piece 29.
- Cut 4 of pattern piece 30.

2. Appliqué the pieces onto the blue background.

FINISHING

1. Layer the quilt top with batting and backing. Baste or pin.

2. Quilt as desired and bind.

CUTTING

Blue fabric

- Cut 1 square 18½″ × 18½″.

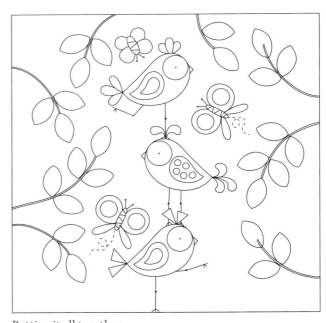

Putting it all together

FLOOZY FLAMINGO

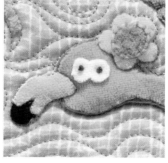

FINISHED WALL QUILT:
14½″ × 14½″

Made by Kim Schaefer,
quilted by Susan Lawson of
Seemingly Slawson Quilts

Floozy is posing in a pond
among the lily pads. The
background fabric is from
my Mesh collection with
Andover Fabrics.

MATERIALS

Fabric

• 1 fat quarter of teal cotton fabric
  for appliqué background

Felted wool

• 1 square 10″ × 10″ of pink
  for flamingo

• 1 square 10″ × 10″ of taupe
  for palm tree trunk

• 1 square 10″ × 10″ of peach
  for flamingo legs

• 1 rectangle 3″ × 14″ of blue
  for water

• 7 squares 5″ × 5″ of assorted
  greens for leaves, grass,
  and lily pads

Felted wool scraps

• 2 pinks for flamingo beak,
  wing, tail, and circles

• 2 yellows for flowers

• Orange for scarf

• Black for beak

• White for eyes

Other

• 18″ × 18″ of batting

• ¾ yard for backing and binding

• 1 yard of paper-backed
  fusible web

• Assorted threads for appliqué
  and embroidery

APPLIQUÉ

1. Refer to Appliqué (page 6) and the Floozy Flamingo appliqué patterns (pages 25–28).

- Cut 1 each of pattern pieces 1–118.
- Cut 2 of pattern piece 119.
- Cut 5 of pattern piece 120.

2. Appliqué the pieces onto the teal background.

FINISHING

1. Layer the quilt top with batting and backing. Baste or pin.

2. Quilt as desired and bind.

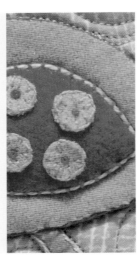

CUTTING

Teal fabric

- Cut 1 square 14½˝ × 14½˝.

Putting it all together

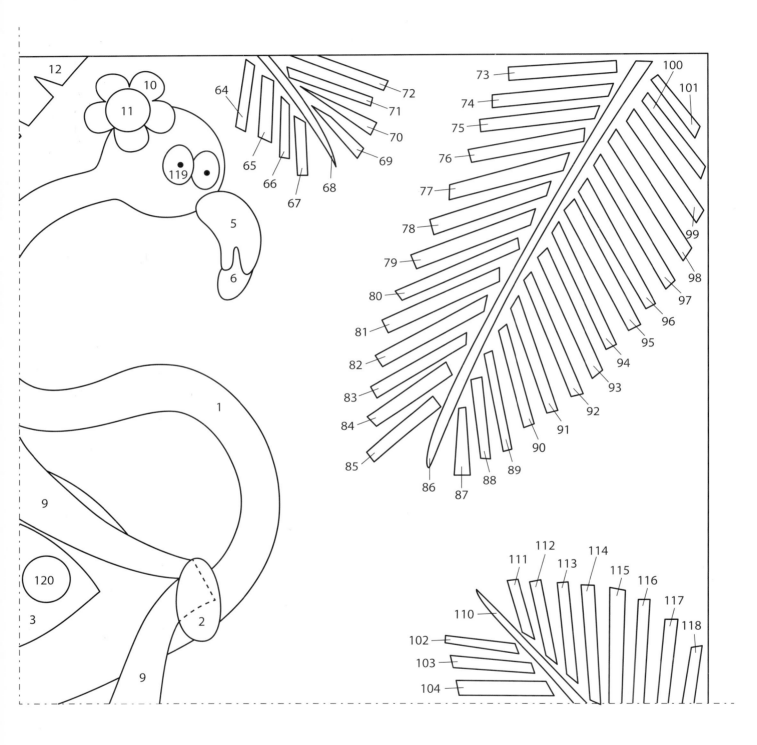

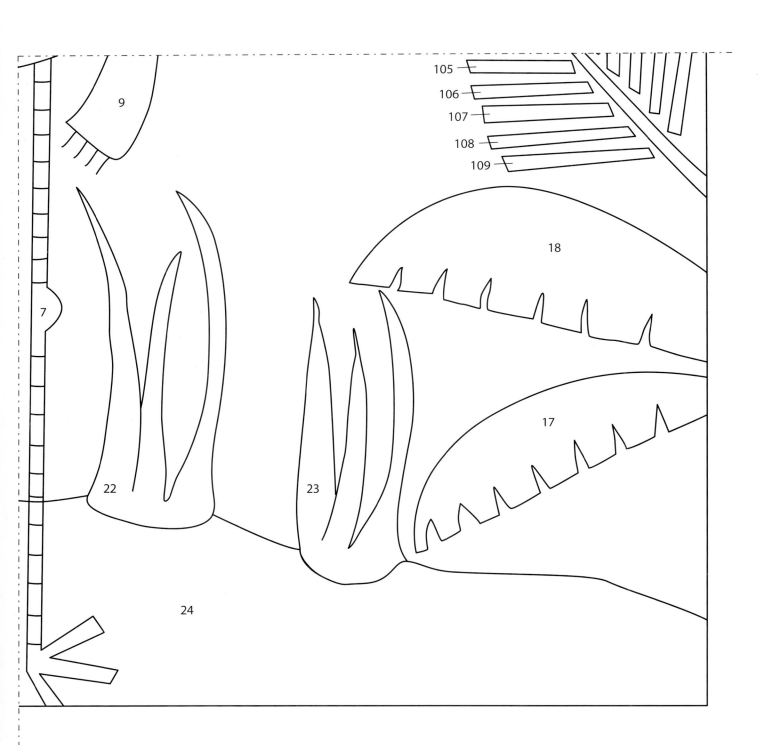

9

105
106
107
108
109

18

7

17

22

23

24

Bright BLOOMS

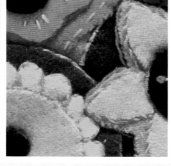

FINISHED WALL QUILT:
14½″ × 14½″

Made by Kim Schaefer, quilted by Susan Lawson of Seamingly Slawson Quilts

This vase of bright blooms is sure to brighten any wall.

MATERIALS

Fabric

- 1 fat quarter of yellow cotton fabric for appliqué background
- 1 fat quarter of red cotton fabric for appliqué background

Felted wool

- 1 square 10″ × 10″ of black for vase and flower centers
- 1 square 10″ × 10″ of white for vase and circles
- 4 squares 5″ × 5″ of assorted greens for flowers

Felted wool scraps

- 5 assorted blues for flowers
- 3 assorted oranges for flowers
- 3 assorted reds for flowers
- 3 assorted purples for flowers
- 5 assorted pinks for flowers
- 2 assorted yellows for flowers
- Teal for flowers

Other

- 18″ × 18″ of batting
- ¾ yard for backing and binding
- 2 yards of paper-backed fusible web
- Assorted threads for appliqué and embroidery

PIECING

Sew the yellow and red strips together for the background. Press.

Piece the background.

APPLIQUÉ

1. Refer to Appliqué (page 6) and the Bright Blooms appliqué patterns (pages 31–34).

• Cut 1 each of pattern pieces 1–67.

• Cut 13 of pattern piece 68.

2. Appliqué the pieces.

FINISHING

1. Layer the quilt top with batting and backing. Baste or pin.

2. Quilt as desired and bind.

CUTTING

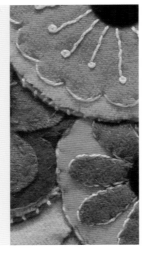

Yellow fabric

• Cut 1 rectangle 14½″ × 10″.

Red fabric

• Cut 1 rectangle 14½″ × 5″.

Putting it all together

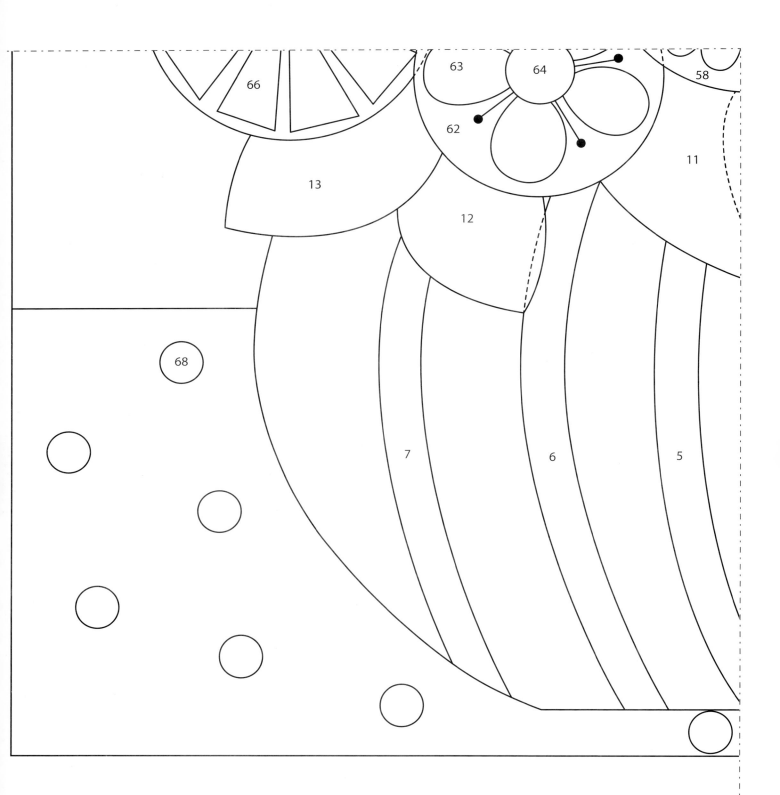

FINISHED QUILT: 16½″ × 16½″

Made by Kim Schaefer, quilted by Susan Lawson of Seamingly Slawson Quilts

This big-eyed fish happily spends his days under the sea swimming among the shells and starfish.

UNDER THE SEA

MATERIALS

Fabric

- 1 fat quarter of blue cotton fabric for background

Felted wool

- 1 square 10″ × 10″ of teal for fish body
- 1 square 10″ × 10″ of purple for fish eye lids, fins, and tail
- 1 square 10″ × 10″ of green for water lily stems and leaves
- 2 squares 10″ × 10″ of assorted greens for center and right-side seaweed
- 1 rectangle 4″ × 15″ of green for left-side seaweed
- 1 square 5″ × 5″ of green for seagrass

- 1 square 5″ × 5″ of coral for water lilies
- 1 square 5″ × 5″ of pink for water lilies

Felted wool scraps

- Blue for bubbles
- White for eyes and shell
- Black for eyes
- 2 oranges for fish mouth and tail
- 2 pinks for fish circles and mouth
- Red for fish circles
- Yellow for starfish

Other

- 20″ × 20″ of batting
- ¾ yard for backing and binding
- ¾ yard of paper-backed fusible web
- Assorted threads for appliqué and embroidery

APPLIQUÉ

1. Refer to Appliqué (page 6) and the Under the Sea appliqué pattern (pullout page P2).

- Cut 1 each of pattern pieces 1–40.
- Cut 3 each of pattern piece 41 and 42.
- Cut 5 each of pattern pieces 43 and 44.

2. Appliqué the pieces onto the blue background.

FINISHING

1. Layer the quilt top with batting and backing. Baste or pin.

2. Quilt as desired and bind.

CUTTING

Blue fabric

- Cut 1 square 16½″ × 16½″.

Putting it all together

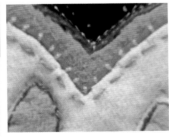

FINISHED WALL QUILT:
10½″ × 10½″

Made by Kim Schaefer,
quilted by Susan Lawson of
Seamingly Slawson Quilts

Heart flowers are stitched
over a pieced background of
fabrics from Giuseppe Ribaudo
(a.k.a. Giucy Giuce). His collection is called Spectrastic from
Andover Fabrics.

Heart Flowers

MATERIALS

Fabric

- ¼ yard total of assorted bright cotton fabrics for pieced background
- 1 fat quarter of black cotton fabric for center of pieced background

Felted wool

- 1 square 10″ × 10″ of pink for heart
- 1 square 10″ × 10″ of light for heart

Felted wool scraps

- Green for stems and leaves
- Pink for heart flowers

Other

- 14″ × 14″ of batting

- ⅓ yard for backing and binding
- ¼ yard paper-backed fusible web
- Assorted threads for appliqué and embroidery

CUTTING

Assorted brights

- Cut 30 rectangles 1½″ × 2″.
- Cut 4 rectangles 2½″ × 2″.
- Cut 2 rectangles 2″ × 3″.
- Cut 2 squares 1½″ × 1½″.
- Cut 2 rectangles 1½″ × 2½″.
- Cut 2 squares 2″ × 2″.

Black fabric

- Cut 1 square 5½″ × 5½″.

PIECING

Sew the black square and bright squares and rectangles together for the background. Press.

APPLIQUÉ

1. Refer to Appliqué (page 6) and the Heart Flowers appliqué pattern (below).

- Cut 1 each of pattern pieces 1–5.
- Cut 3 of pattern piece 6.
- Cut 6 of pattern piece 7.

2. Appliqué the pieces onto the pieced background.

FINISHING

1. Layer the quilt top with batting and backing. Baste or pin.

2. Quilt as desired and bind.

Piece the background.

1½"×2"	1½"×2"	1½"×2"	1½"×1½"	1½"×2"	1½"×2"	1½"×2"	
1½"×2"	1½"×2"	1½"×2"	2½"×2"	1½"×2"	1½"×2"	2½"×2"	1½"×2"

Left-side pieces: 1½"×2", 2"×2", 1½"×2½", 1½"×2", 2"×3", 1½"×2"

Center: 5½"×5½"

Right-side pieces: 2"×2", 1½"×2", 1½"×2", 1½"×2½", 2"×3", 1½"×2"

1½"×2"	2½"×2"	1½"×2"	1½"×2"	2½"×2"	1½"×2"	1½"×2"	1½"×2"
1½"×2"	1½"×2"	1½"×2"	1½"×1½"	1½"×2"	1½"×2"	1½"×2"	

THE NEIGHBORHOOD

FINISHED WALL QUILT:
16½″ × 16½″

Made by Kim Schaefer,
quilted by Susan Lawson of
Seamingly Slawson Quilts

Three houses sit on the top
of a hill filled with flowers.
The pieced border is made
using Alison Glass's collection with Andover Fabrics
called Chroma.

MATERIALS

Fabric

- 1 fat quarter of blue cotton fabric for background
- ¼ yard total of assorted bright cotton fabrics for pieced border

Felted wool

- 1 rectangle 8″ × 12½″ of green for grass

Felted wool scraps

- 4 assorted yellows for sun, door, house, and flower
- 3 assorted purples for roof, house, and flower
- 3 assorted oranges for chimneys, door, and flower
- 3 assorted reds for house and flowers
- 3 assorted blues for roof and flower
- 3 assorted pinks for door, flowers, and small flowers
- 2 assorted teals for flower
- White felted wool for windows and cloud
- 5 assorted greens for roof and leaves

Other

- 20″ × 20″ of batting
- ¾ yard for backing and binding
- 1 yard paper-backed fusible web
- Assorted threads for appliqué and embroidery

BORDERS

1. Sew together 6 assorted bright squares for each of the 2 side borders.

Piece 2 side borders.

2. Sew the side borders to the quilt top. Press.

3. Sew together 8 assorted bright squares for each of the top and bottom borders. Press.

Piece top and bottom borders.

4. Sew the top and bottom borders to the quilt top. Press.

FINISHING

1. Layer the quilt top with batting and backing. Baste or pin.

2. Quilt as desired and bind.

Putting it all together

CUTTING

Blue fabric

• Cut 1 square 12½″ × 12½″.

Assorted brights

• Cut 28 squares 2½″ × 2½″.

APPLIQUÉ

1. Refer to Appliqué (page 6) and The Neighborhood appliqué patterns (pages 41–44).

• Cut 1 each of pattern pieces 1–31.

• Cut 9 of pattern piece 32.

• Cut 4 each of pattern pieces 33 and 34.

• Cut 8 of pattern piece 35.

• Cut 12 of pattern piece 36.

• Cut 7 each of pattern pieces 37 and 38.

2. Appliqué the quilt onto the blue background.

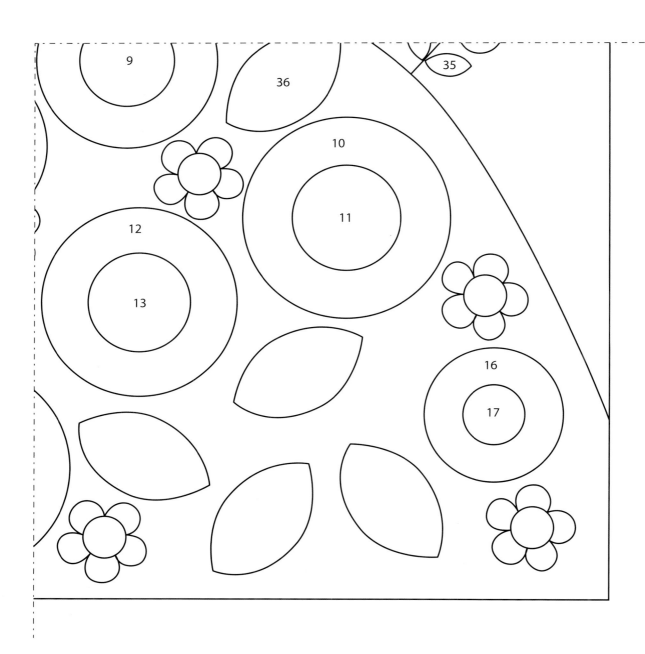

Cool Cotton & Whimsical Wool Quilts

FLOWER FESTIVAL

FINISHED WALL QUILT:
20½″ × 20½″

Made by Kim Schaefer, quilted by Susan Lawson of Seamingly Slawson Quilts

Butterflies, bees, a ladybug, and a caterpillar frolic among this colorful whimsical garden.

MATERIALS

Fabric

- 1 fat quarter of light blue cotton fabric for background
- ¼ yard total of assorted bright cotton fabrics for pieced border

Felted wool

- 1 square 10″ × 10″ of orange for flower and caterpillar
- 1 square 5″ × 5″ of rust for flower
- 1 square 5″ × 5″ of gold for flower
- 1 square 5″ × 5″ of medium yellow for flower
- 1 square 5″ × 5″ of pink for flower
- 1 rectangle 1¾″ × 10″ of green for stem and leaves
- 1 rectangle 1¾″ × 6″ of green for stem and leaves
- 1 rectangle 1¾″ × 5½″ of green for stem and leaves
- 1 rectangle 1¾″ × 12″ of green for stem and leaves
- 1 rectangle 1¾″ × 10½″ of green for stem, leaves, and caterpillar

Felted wool scraps

- 3 assorted purples for butterfly
- 3 assorted blues for butterfly and flower
- 3 assorted teals for butterfly
- Bright yellow for flower and bee bodies
- Orange for flower
- 2 assorted peaches for flower
- Red for flower and ladybug
- 2 assorted pinks for flower
- White for bee wings

Other

- 24″ × 24″ of batting
- ¾ yard for backing and binding
- 1 yard paper-backed fusible web
- Assorted threads for appliqué and embroidery

BORDERS

1. Sew together 8 squares for each of the 2 side borders. Press.

Piece 2 side borders.

2. Sew the 2 side borders to the quilt top. Press.

3. Sew together 10 squares for each of the top and bottom borders. Press.

Piece top and bottom borders.

4. Sew the top and bottom borders to the quilt top. Press.

FINISHING

1. Layer the quilt top with batting and backing. Baste or pin.

2. Quilt as desired and bind.

CUTTING

Light blue fabric

• Cut 1 square 16½″ × 16½″.

Assorted brights

• Cut 36 squares 2½″ × 2½″.

APPLIQUÉ

1. Refer to Appliqué (page 6) and the Flower Festival appliqué patterns (pages 47–50).

• Cut 1 each of pattern pieces 1–29.

• Cut 3 each of pattern pieces 30–37.

• Cut 8 pattern pieces 38.

• Cut 6 each of pattern pieces 39 and 40.

• Cut 1 and 1 reverse of pattern piece 41.

2. Appliqué the pieces onto the blue background.

Putting it all together

FINISHED QUILT: 17½″ × 17½″

Made by Kim Schaefer,
quilted by Susan Lawson of
Seamingly Slawson Quilts

Three owls perched on a
tree with butterflies, flowers,
a frog, and mushrooms. The
border stripe is one of my
favorite stripes I designed
with Andover Fabrics.

THree on a Tree

MATERIALS

Fabric

- 1 fat quarter of light teal cotton
  fabric for background
- ⅛ yard of black tone-on-tone
  cotton fabric for inner border
- ¼ yard of stripe cotton fabric
  for outer border

Felted wool

- 1 square 12″ × 12″ of brown
  for tree
- 2 squares 5″ × 5″ of 2 green for
  frog, flower stems, and leaves

Felted wool scraps

- 4 blues for owl
- 4 pinks for owl

- 4 purples for owl
- 2 yellows for butterfly
- 2 oranges for butterfly, beaks, and feet
- 2 corals for tulips
- 2 reds for mushroom tops
- Black for butterfly bodies and owl eyes
- White for owl eyes, frog eyes,
  mushroom stems, and spots
- Green for leaves

Other

- 21″ × 21″ of batting
- ¾ yard for backing and binding
- 1 yard paper-backed fusible web
- Assorted threads for appliqué
  and embroidery

- Cut 3 each of pattern pieces 16–28.
- Cut 6 each of pattern pieces 29 and 30.
- Cut 8 of pattern piece 31.
- Cut 66 of pattern piece 32.
- Cut 1 and 1 reverse of pattern piece 33.

2. Appliqué the pieces onto the light teal background.

BORDERS

1. Refer to the Putting It All Together diagram (below).

2. Sew the 2 side inner borders to the quilt top. Press.

3. Sew top and bottom inner borders to the quilt top. Press.

4. Sew the 2 side outer borders to the quilt top. Press.

5. Sew top and bottom outer borders to the quilt top. Press.

FINISHING

1. Layer the quilt top with batting and backing. Baste or pin.

2. Quilt as desired and bind.

CUTTING

Light teal fabric

- Cut 1 square 12½″ × 12½″

Black fabric

- Cut 2 strips 1¼″ × 12½″ for 2 side inner borders.
- Cut 2 strips 1¼″ × 14″ for top and bottom inner borders.

Stripe fabric

- Cut 2 strips 2¼″ × 14″ for 2 side outer borders.
- Cut 2 strips 2¼ × 17½″ for top and bottom outer borders.

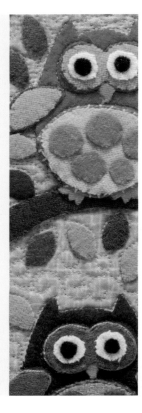

APPLIQUÉ

1. Refer to Appliqué (page 6) and the Three on a Tree appliqué patterns (pages 53–56).

- Cut 1 each of pattern pieces 1–9.
- Cut 2 each of pattern pieces 10–15.

Putting it all together

TULIP MEDALLION

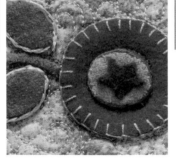

FINISHED QUILT: $18\frac{1}{2}″ \times 18\frac{1}{2}″$

Made by Kim Schaefer, quilted by Susan Lawson of Seamingly Slawson Quilts

This little medallion is created with purples, greens and black. That combination of colors has always been one of my favorites to work with.

MATERIALS

Fabric

- 1 fat quarter of bright purple cotton fabric for medallion center
- ⅛ yard of green cotton fabric for pieced borders
- ⅛ yard of black cotton fabric for corner squares
- ⅛ yard of light purple cotton fabric for outer pieced borders
- ⅛ yard of dark purple cotton fabric for outer pieced borders

Felted wool

- 3 squares 10″ × 10″ of 3 purple for tulips, circles, and stars
- 3 squares 5″ × 5″ of 3 green for stems and leaves

Other

- 22″ × 22″ of batting
- ¾ yard for backing and binding
- 1 yard paper-backed fusible web
- Assorted threads for appliqué and embroidery

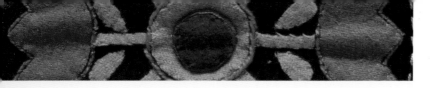

CUTTING

Bright purple fabric
- Cut 1 square 8½″ × 8½″.

Green fabric
- Cut 4 rectangles 3½″ × 8½″.

Black fabric
- Cut 4 squares 3½″ × 3½″.

Light purple fabric
- Cut 16 squares 2½″ × 2½″.

Dark purple fabric
- Cut 16 squares 2½″ × 2½″.

PIECING

Arrange and sew together the bright purple, green, and black background pieces to form the quilt top. Press.

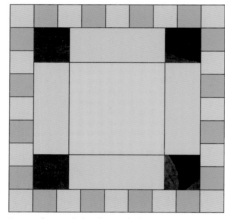

Piece the quilt background.

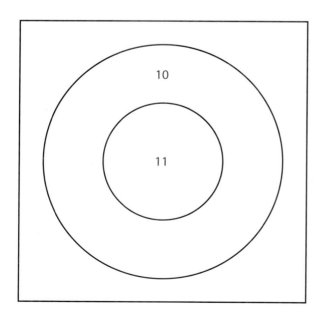

APPLIQUÉ

1. Refer to Appliqué (page 6) and Tulip Medallion appliqué patterns (below left and next page).

Block A (Tulips):
- Cut 8 each of pattern pieces 1 and 2.
- Cut 4 each of pattern pieces 3–7.
- Cut 1 each of pattern pieces 8 and 9.

Block B (Corner Blocks):
- Cut 4 each of pattern pieces 10 and 11.

Block C (Border Rectangle):
- Cut 4 each of pattern pieces 12–16.
- Cut 24 of pattern piece 17.

2. Appliqué the blocks to the pieced background.

BORDERS

1. Sew together 4 light purple squares and 3 dark purple squares for each of the 2 side borders.

2. Sew the side borders to the quilt top. Press.

3. Sew together 4 light purple squares and 5 dark purple squares for the top and bottom borders.

4. Sew the top and bottom borders to the quilt top. Press.

FINISHING

1. Layer the quilt top with batting and backing. Baste or pin.

2. Quilt as desired and bind.

Putting it all together

SPOTTED POTS

FINISHED QUILT: 40½″ × 40½″
FINISHED BLOCK: 8″ × 8″

Made by Kim Schaefer,
quilted by Susan Lawson of
Seamingly Slawson Quilts

Nine bright flower pots are framed by a black-and-white border.

MATERIALS

Fabric

- 1 yard of black tone-on-tone cotton fabric for appliqué block backgrounds
- ⅔ yard of black-on-white print cotton fabric for horizontal and vertical lattice
- ⅝ yard of white-on-black print cotton fabric for pieced border

Felted wool

- 1 square 10″ × 10″ and 2 squares 5″ × 5″ of assorted purples for flowers, pots, and circles
- 1 square 10″ × 10″ and 3 squares 5″ × 5″ of assorted oranges and rusts for flowers, pots, and circles
- 1 square 10″ × 10″ and 4 squares 5″ × 5″ of assorted yellows and golds for flowers, pots, and circles
- 1 square 10″ × 10″ and 4 squares 5″ × 5″ of assorted pinks for flowers, pots, and circles
- 3 squares 5″ × 5″ of assorted teals for flowers and circles
- 2 squares 10″ × 10″ and 3 squares 5″ × 5″ of assorted blues for flowers, pots, and circles
- 1 square 10″ × 10″ and 2 squares 5″ × 5″ of assorted reds for flowers, pots, and circles
- 1 square 10″ × 10″ and 4 squares 5″ × 5″ of assorted greens for pots and leaves
- 1 square 10″ × 10″ of white for spots on pots

Other

- 46″ × 46″ of batting
- 2½ yards for backing and binding
- 3 yards paper-backed fusible web
- Assorted threads for appliqué and embroidery

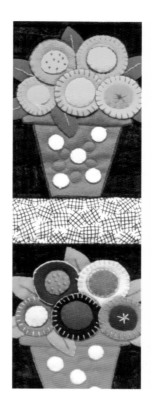

CUTTING

Black fabric

- Cut 9 squares 9½″ × 9½″. (Trim to 8½″ × 8½″ after appliqué and embroidery are complete.)
- Cut 16 squares 3½″ × 3½″. (Trim to 2½″ × 2½″ after appliqué and embroidery are complete.)

Black-on-white fabric

- Cut 24 rectangles 2½″ × 8½″.
- Cut 16 rectangles 2½″ × 4½″.

White-on-black fabric

- Cut 4 squares 4½″ × 4½″.
- Cut 12 rectangles 4½″ × 8½″.

APPLIQUÉ

1. Refer to Appliqué (page 6) and the Spotted Pots appliqué patterns (below right and next page).

For each of the 9 blocks:

• Cut 1 each of pattern pieces 1–17.

• Cut 5 of pattern piece 18.

For cornerstones:

• Cut 16 of pattern piece 19.

2. Appliqué pieces 1–18 onto the black 9½″ × 9½″ squares. (Trim to 8½″ × 8½″.)

3. Appliqué piece 19 onto the black 3½″ × 3½″ squares. (Trim to 2½″ × 2½″.)

PIECING

1. Arrange the blocks in 3 rows of 3 blocks each.

2. Sew the vertical lattice between the blocks and on each end of the row. Sew the outer border pieces to each end of the row.

Piece flower-block rows. Make 3 rows.

3. Arrange the circle squares in 4 rows of 4 circles each. Sew the horizontal lattice pieces between the circle squares and add a short lattice strip on each end of the row. Press.

Piece horizontal lattice rows. Make 4 rows.

4. Piece the top and bottom outer borders using the border squares, short lattice strips, and border strips. Press.

Piece top and bottom borders.

5. Arrange and sew the rows together. Press.

FINISHING

1. Layer the quilt top with batting and backing. Baste or pin.

2. Quilt as desired and bind.

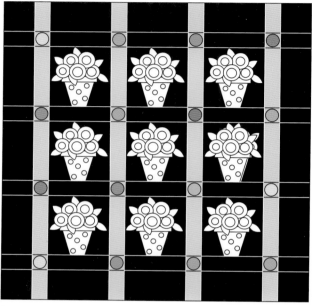

Putting it all together

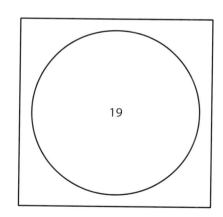

ABOUT THE AUTHOR

Kim Schaefer began sewing at an early age and was quilting seriously by the late 1980s. Her early quilting career included designing and producing small quilts for craft shows and shops across the country.

In 1996 Kim founded Little Quilt Company, a pattern company focused on designing a variety of small, fun-to-make projects.

In addition to designing quilt patterns, Kim is a best-selling author for C&T Publishing. Kim also designs fabric for Andover Fabrics.

Kim lives with her family in southeastern Wisconsin.

Visit Kim online and follow on social media!

Website: littlequiltcompany.com
See Kim's entire collection of patterns, books, and fabrics!

Facebook: Little Quilt Company
See posts about new patterns, books, and fabrics and an occasional peek at Kim's latest work!

ALSO BY KIM SCHAEFER:

 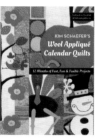